A Home Is Not Always Where The Heart Is

Memories are our
most precious gift &
love our greatest light.
Best- Denise
Martinson

A Home Is Not Always Where The Heart Is

Denise Martinson

Writers Club Press
New York Lincoln Shanghai

A Home Is Not Always Where The Heart Is

All Rights Reserved © 2003 by Denise Martinson

No part of this book may be reproduced or transmitted in any form or by any means, graphic, electronic, or mechanical, including photocopying, recording, taping, or by any information storage retrieval system, without the written permission of the publisher.

Writers Club Press
an imprint of iUniverse, Inc.

For information address:
iUniverse, Inc.
2021 Pine Lake Road, Suite 100
Lincoln, NE 68512
www.iuniverse.com

Illustration copyright by Anthony DeMaggio
All Rights Reserved. Copyright © 2003

ISBN: 0-595-26731-9

Printed in the United States of America

To my mother, Florence, and my father, Daniel: You both have given me the inspiration to forge ahead and reap the rewards that make dreams come true. Without dreams, no life, no truth in our inner selves, could shape us to go on to be the best that we can be. Thank you for your love and guidance and for telling me to follow my heart.

To Mike, Danielle, Michael, Danny, and Cathie—my family, my life. I love you all.

To Edie and Jeannine for being there for my mother and I when we needed additional support at the most difficult times.

God does answer prayers. I know because he gave me all of you.

Contents

List of Illustrations xi

Believe I xiii

Preface xv

Young At Heart xvii

Introduction xix

Mrs. Jackson's Journal Entry 3

Ring Around The Rosie 5

Mom I 6

What Matters Most 7

Food Wars 13

Where Memory Lives 14

Laughter Is The Best Medicine 15

Our Summer Barbecue 16

You Are My Sunshine 19

For Husband George In Room 214 20

More To Puzzles Than Their Answers 22

Life In Its Simplicity 26

Wedding Day Farewell 27

Home Sickness 28

Where Is It, Where Is It? 31

Steve is Not John, Or Is He 32

A Home Is Not Always Where The Heart Is

Mom II	33
Stage Three	34
Mrs. Jackson's Journal Entry	37
The Ghost of Uncle Jim	39
Visiting Isn't So Bad	40
Castaways	42
Fair Game, No Gain	43
Rhinestones Are A Girl's Best Friend	44
Who Says You Shouldn't Smoke	47
Love Letter To My Wife	49
An Aide In Need	53
Father Hangs In Chandler Hall	55
Nurse Katherine On Dementia	56
Vigil	57
Mother Said There Would Be Days Like This	61
Few Visitors, Fewer Friends	62
Mrs. Jackson's Journal Entry	65
Day In And Day Out	67
Safe From The Outside World	68
Once More In Winter	69
Andrew Sees The Light	73
Right Temporal Lobe	75
It's All In The Heart	76
We Watch, We Wonder, We Wait No More	78
An Apple A Day	81
Over Developed	82
It's A Matter of Time	83
Mrs. Jackson's Journal Entry	87

Contents

Hard Facts, Harder Truths 90
Bath Wars 91
Believe II 95
Mom III 96
What Are They Thinking? 98
For Every Tree That Grows 100
Future World—2090 101
It's All Relative 103
Mrs. Jackson's Journal Entry 104
Andrew Sees More Light 109
Emily Recites A Holiday Poem 111
Afterthoughts 112
On Seeing My Husband In A Nursing Home 113
Dr. Skip's Prescription 114
Family Dinner Day 117
Home For New Years 118
Mom IV 123
Song For Pops 124
Nursing Home Care 125
A Home Is Not Always Where The Heart Is 126

Afterwords 129
A Cure Soon 133
About the Author 135

List of Illustrations

By Anthony DeMaggio

Mrs. Jackson With Her Walker……………………………………….. 9

Randy Stuffing His Face……………………………………………… 58

Mom In Her Sweater…………………………………………………. 70

Frank and Tim Playing Checkers……………………………………... 84

Agnes With Her Baby Doll…………………………………………… 120

    Anthony DeMaggio is an illustrator and computer artist who lives in Sterling Heights, MI. Anthony received his bachelors degree in Fine Arts/Illustration from The College for Creative Studies in Detroit, MI.

Believe I

When you are ready to go out into the world spread love and courage, so others will always find strength and understanding to embrace wisdom through tranquility and serenity. Try to understand the troubled, and give them your hand and warm smile to brighten their day. Walk proud and lift your head in the face of adversity. Be optimistic and see good in all things, and remember in your heart of hearts—even if you do not believe in God, He believes in you.

Preface

After my mother was placed into a nursing home, I almost hated visiting her because it was hard watching her so helpless, and that I had to walk away and leave her with strangers tore at my heart each time I left the Home. The truth is I felt guilty. But the more I visited her, the more I could feel the guilt dissolve inside, and by listening to some of the other residents relate their stories and feelings, I saw how much they needed visitors who cared about them. It helped ease my mind, and yet it also taught me a great deal about myself.

I remember when I used to think that nursing homes were depressing, that they smelled of urine and seemed dark and unwelcoming. They were, to a point, until I saw how clean and bright the well-attended ones were, and how their well-trained staff worked together so the residents could have a Home away from home in all aspects of their lives. It was really the start of my need to write this book.

After getting to know the routines and the men and women who live with my mother, I wanted them to get to know me as well. After many worthwhile visits, their worries and anxieties subsided, and I could relax and interact easier without feeling like I was intruding on their lives. It was a comfortable setting as we shared quality time singing and laughing together.

Being with them taught me that they are still human beings worth caring about, because as I state throughout the book, we, too, may have to resort to these facilities—whether assisted living or nursing homes—and to think that we could lose our dignity in the face of it all, can be an eye-opener to those who say, "Nursing Homes are so depressing." In fact, looking at the aged is like looking in a mirror. Their reflection is our reflection.

A Home Is Not Always Where The Heart Is is not a serious look at the aged, nor a journal filled with information on why a person develops Alzheimer's disease. Rather it is an honest look—through humor and the day-to-day living of the aged in a home.

This is why I wrote the book—to give others a look at what some care facilities are really like and what some of the residents go through. But, more than that, to dispel the half-truths that all homes are unworthy of the residents who live inside them. They deserve more than that.

I want to thank the residents who shared their lives and colorful stories with me; the aides who took the time to explain and inform me about my mother's care; the nurses responsible for the more important phone calls regarding the good and bad days Mom endured through her dementia; the new acquaintances I met whose family members reside at the Home; and most especially, the support of family and friends who never wavered in the toughest of times when we almost lost her.

I will miss those residents who shared their lives with me before passing on, especially Katy—whose smile can still be seen in each and every face at the Home.

Young At Heart

Those who continue to think young
stay young. We are told
to remain active throughout life.
Perhaps for most, not I
caught between wind and rain,
no safe harbor to hide in.
Exercise and healthy food a must,
disease directs me otherwise.
Keep spirit and hope and faith alive,
be strong as tempered steel.

Introduction

Visiting a nursing home gives us hope and opens our sometimes closed minds with the stark realization that we need to establish a connection, and to look at what is really happening, look at ourselves, and maybe just maybe we can understand.

In the following pages of short prose and poetry, I have touched on the feelings and stories told through the eyes of nurses, aides, and the resident-patients in journal form, so we can feel as though we are sitting next to them as they relate their experiences through their day-to-day existence in *Spirit Care Home* for the aged. We can learn from their sense of humor, their fears and worries, and their pain if we listen to what they have to say.

Those who receive care in other facilities most likely share these same feelings and stories I present here, and perhaps those of us not yet old, will speak out to those lawmakers who are able to take another look at health care and social services, for they, too, will one day need the support and understanding when and if they find themselves in the same situation.

Through it all, the laughter and the tears, the inevitable staring you straight in the face, and the aides and nurses who work tirelessly, often overtime, yet still respectful through crisis, still smiling, even passionate about their jobs, deserves mention.

Besides reading about those who find themselves behind the doors of the aged and what they experience, I believe we all need to take some time out from our own busy schedules to visit a nursing home or assisted living facility. Many of the residents never receive visitors, and to see their eyes light up or a smile cross their face is such a rewarding experience. A kind word or a simple gesture like bringing them flowers or magazines can make a difference for all of us.

There is no sugarcoating, and as you read through the pages, hopefully, you will experience frustration, contentment, reassurance, courage, love, and most important of all, truth.

(I have changed the names and the name of the Home, and even though what you are about to read is, in fact, truth, I have embellished some of their stories to protect the rights of the individual.)

We need to pray in the quiet of our hearts because this is where God promised to meet us.

A Home Is Not Always Where The Heart Is

Mrs. Jackson's Journal Entry
My hospital meeting with other patients for Nursing Home Transfer (June 12, 2001)

Morning:

As I straightened my back and flexed my knees, to relieve the cramped feeling in my legs, I saw the tallest head emerge from a small group of doctors, and attached to the head was Dr. Skip's skinny, undernourished body (worse than some of ours) stand up. Although, it was hard for me to see the other patients because I was at the far side of the room, I had no trouble picking him out. His shock of black hair looked as slippery as a slicked-up bowling ball.

I had to laugh as he took the three steps of the platform in one stride. The more I studied him, the more he reminded me of a parking meter, waiting to be fed. I know it's not nice to say, I used to like him before my diagnosis, but I felt I had an enemy now, threatening me with his orders—along with my family's—that I had to be admitted into a nursing home. I didn't like the way it made me feel.

He gave his little speech, if that's what you call it—telling us we would receive the best of care, and then it was time to leave.

Through the group of chairs, I saw several nurses hurrying over to where we sat. I was glad nurse Johnson—always a friendly child—stuck out her hand to lift me up. At least with her helping me, I wouldn't look like such a clod. I have my pride. "Easy does it, Mrs. Jackson. Are you ready to go?"

"I suppose," I said, eyeing Dr. Skip

But right now I didn't feel like balking. Secretly, I wished that I could roll myself into a huge ball and soar across the room and disappear forever. Who wants to be taken away from their home? Just because I can't do the things I used to any longer…but I guess I have no choice.

The last thing I saw when I left the room were smiles on the doctors' faces. I wonder if they would still smile if they were the ones going to live in an old folks' home.

Afternoon:

After we arrived I was wheeled under a banner, which announced, "Welcome to Spirit Care Home" in bold, black letters. Other residents filed in through the side entrance, and aides and nurses were milling around, directing them like traffic cops. Some of the oldies were hurrying to get the best seats—the ones not in wheelchairs. I don't see why. It was only a welcoming committee for old people. It wasn't as if they were getting prizes for heaven's sake.

I have decided to give this place a chance. They serve really good food, and I guess some of the activities they have planned for us could be fun. Just as long as Dr. Skippy peanut butter doesn't find something else wrong with me, I'll put up with it. Besides, I became friends with a few of the ladies here. It could be worse.

Ring Around The Rosie

Those nights I sat with my mother,
her bone-hugging arms held tight
her memories, while I, her son,
provide no shield from dementia days:
Her distorted view of faces,
fade in and out unfocused
like smoke-wrapped clouds.
She sits in cluttered corner still
unraveling tight-stitched shawl she made
in other days when life was young.
When happy memories filled her
with whimsical fairy-taled existence,
where family gathered in laughter
and children circled to sing and dance
to "Ring around the Rosie."

Now her browning years are turned to stone.
No starry-eyed dreams are left to hold.
And I, proud son, hear echoed words
consumed by the fire-light glow:
"Ashes! Ashes! We all fall down."

Mom I
(daughter speaks)

I was fortunate in finding a well-kept nursing home for my mother whose Alzheimer's symptoms were steadily increasing. After a week of moving to *Spirit Care Home's* Chandler Hall where the Alzheimer patients—in the early stages of their disease—were housed, the head nurse advised moving her to Station II (the medicare and medicaid area) because they felt she needed extended care beyond what they were able to give her. This seemed the perfect place for her condition, and soon a temporary room was set up.

She, at first, balked at taking her medication, and eventually caught a cold, then refused to eat. It wasn't long before the facility recommended I contact hospice. Thankfully, after prayer and continued support, her outlook changed dramatically, and the need for hospice was halted. She began eating again, walking, and became more alert instead of constantly sleeping.

Once again she was moved.

In her present room, which suits her even more, she sits by the window gazing out at the flowered lawn, the sun shining on her thin face, making her almost look ten years younger. Her eyes light up and the smile on her face dispels my own sense of sadness as the memories she tries so hard to remember somehow unfold themselves in her simple words. She tells me she is happy, that is enough for now.

What Matters Most

They sit in wheelchairs,
eyes on plates, their faces
as still as their thoughts.
Two mouthfuls, sometimes more
are lifted to lips, their
grateful nods or indifference
in plain view.

Sprinkled aides wipe mouths,
visitors twist in chairs;
their nervous hands rub backs
for reassurance, yet gently scold,
"You must eat or you'll get sick."
Their eyes reject our pleas.

These empty words are cast aside
like yesterday's leftovers.
Frustration attaches to enter hearts,
"tapping into" reality.

It is natural getting old.
It is natural we worry.
They say we're only human.

In time
Love is the link designed
to reassure connection.
Faith emanates light.

A Home Is Not Always Where The Heart Is

Strength, being so strong,
brings hope…God.

A Home Is Not Always Where The Heart Is

Mrs. Jackson with her walker

In order to be healthy, it is our spirit that first needs to be cleaned, then rinsed with pure water.

Food Wars

Some of the aides called Randy, "the human garbage disposal." The more food he ate, the more he wanted. He never seemed to get full, and today was no exception.

The minute his plate was empty, he reached across the table and snatched Ellen's jello from her tray. Ellen, however, poked at her potatoes and never noticed Randy's quick hands until her fork dug into his finger during his second try at taking her chicken.

Mashed potatoes and jello flew all over the table. The chicken landed in Florence's lap on the other side of the room, and a visitor's head felt the roll. Once Ellen realized what Randy was up to, she screamed, thinking the red jello stemmed from Randy's hands.

"What you'd go and do that for, cuttin' your hand like that on my food?"

Poor Randy just sat there licking the jello from his fingers; Florence thought there were flying chickens in the room; and the visitor thought Florence tossed the roll.

"Do you have anymore potatoes?" Randy asked Ellen.

"What! So you can kill them, too!" she yelled, wiping her mouth with her napkin.

Squinting to see if there was going to be a fight, one of the aides hurried over to the table and quickly took Randy by the arm and led him out of the room. Gently taking him to a nearby seat, the aide told him that he could eat later. Randy, of course, didn't seem to mind. For that matter neither did Ellen who sat watching to see if Randy would come back into the room and steal her last piece of chicken.

This was a typical day for Randy, and as for Florence, she never did find out if chickens could fly.

Where Memory Lives

You are blessed with intelligence,
and each new day only strengthens
that which you lose
and that which you find
in the eyes and heart
you know so well.

What triumphs you keep as you hold
your children and your wife
in arms worth holding.
Arms that warm against the drafts
and the ghosts of yesterday.

You retain much more
than you'll ever know, father:
a memory as strong as you are,
only hidden in a special place
that is always with you…always
a part of your very soul.

Why do I, who has never
felt your loss or your pain,
say this to you now.
Because you remember
to love.

A Home Is Not Always Where The Heart Is

Laughter Is The Best Medicine

"Suicide! But why does she want to do that?" one of the residents asked sitting at the other end of the lunch table.

Depression is why. A whopping 70 percent of the aged get depressed while residing in a nursing home, and Katy is no exception.

She is a slim woman who loves to talk about her past, and most especially, about her children and her job. She would spend time reminiscing about the tricks she played on her coworkers at the plastic factory. She loved to laugh. She loved life. But, this particular day she wanted desperately to go home.

Julie, one of the aides, relayed that this was a common occurrence with Katy, and what they generally did was let her rest on her bed. It usually helped, and she would get up later in the day and act as though nothing had happened.

Katy sat at the table crying and rubbing her eyes. "I want to go home to Chicago. I don't want to live anymore." Julie quickly told her to think about all the wonderful activities the Home had planned for everyone, and how later they would share a movie together. But Katy would have none of it. "I really do," she pleaded as the tears made her cheeks look like shiny rubber.

In the meantime, Mrs. Kranz, the organ player came into the room before lunch and quickly had everyone singing. It put a small smile on Katy's face before she told the aide she had to go to the bathroom. Julie told her that lunch would be waiting and made her promise to come back. When she returned a few minutes later, her eyes were dry. The aide looked her straight in the face, smiled and said, "See! Your tears are gone. You peed them out. Now all the water in your eyes has left your body—from head to toe."

Those must have been the magic words because she burst out laughing. The old Katy was back.

A Home Is Not Always Where The Heart Is

Our Summer Barbecue

The french fries sizzle, golden brown—
crispy like fresh-packed crackerjacks.
The steaks charred over blue flames,
Sauce—red—garlic blend to taste.
Over easy as salad trims our checkered
table cloth. Sweet smell
of apple cider irritates the bees,
puckers lips, as if they weren't
puckered enough.
A light breeze sails napkins
across the yard…scatters.
All our chairs are full as we are,
consumed as flies flirt. Soon, our
contented bellies burp yawns
after pleasant evening memories
of earlier picnics put us to sleep.

If we keep our prayer hands crossed, miracles do happen.

You Are My Sunshine

After watching George and Fay sing, Sherry stood up and placed her knitting on a nearby end table. Her eyes took in their every move. "We're gonna call you both the Gene Kelly and Debbie Reynolds of the Old Folks' Home," she told them clapping along with the other residents and aides.

"I miss the good old days when I used to sing on the stage," George told her as he joined Fay in singing, "You are my sunshine, my only sunshine…" Then George added, teasing them, "Fay here is my best gal."

Not only does Fay love to sing, and her lovely voice blends perfectly with his, but she also has a crush on George. She flirts with most of the male aides and even pinched Philip (her favorite aide) on his behind the other day.

Sherry, on the other hand, can't stand men. If one of them sits near her, she moves to the other side of the room. Either she is playing hard to get, or she likes to be chased because someone caught her winking at Philip when he brought her a magazine to read. Could be she thinks he is her grandson.

The phone rang; Philip answered it. "Be right there, sir. I'm listening to some really good music," he said as he winked at George.

Sherry reached for her knitting, nodded her head and smiled.

"You are my sunshine, my only sunshine."

It is good to see some of the residents doing the things they enjoy most—such as read, knit, watch television, do crossword puzzles, and paint or draw pictures. However, most of them are not able to do the things they used to because of their health. This is why singing and listening to music is such a spirit builder for all of us, and especially for Fay and George.

A Home Is Not Always Where The Heart Is

For Husband George In Room 214
(by wife, a new poet, age 85 in room 202)

I loved you when the willows
swept the land where we sat,
when the birds sang in the wind
and carried our song to the sky.
I loved you as the flowers
swayed to the music we played
each time we wrote the words.
And in the fire-light glow
by the pale moonlight,
I treasure your sparkling eyes;
the way you tilt your head
to kiss my cheek,
and the touch of your hand
when we said our vows.

I loved you when the rain
washed the sand from our clothes,
when the melody still played in our hearts.
I loved you as the years
gently rocked us to sleep
(even now)
in the warmth of our bed
by the carpet of green.
I'll treasure you by my side,
remembering
the way you smile at me
to give me hope
and the touch of your hand

A Home Is Not Always Where The Heart Is

when we say good night
and go our separate ways.

    Love, Millie

More To Puzzles Than Their Answers

Mom carried the birthday present we had for Grandpa to the nursing home. She used to visit him more often, but since my father died he became more withdrawn, which I think is a large part of my problem with him.

When we finally entered his room, he was sitting in his favorite rocking chair, wearing a baseball cap and working a crossword puzzle. He loved working them, and often remarked that a person who could finish a hard one in half an hour was a genius.

"Hi, Gramps," Mom said, as she bent to kiss his forehead.

"What are you doing here?" he answered.

"We brought you a birthday gift. Did you forget today is your birthday?"

He sat there and stared at us. "Who cares. It's just another day. Besides, I'm not in the mood for presents."

I knew Mom tried her best whenever she talked to Grandpa; but because he's so stubborn, it was impossible.

"Please open your gift, Grandpa," I said.

"I don't have the time. I'm doing this puzzle," he replied. "Just go home, the both of you."

"All right, then do your puzzle," I yelled as I stormed out of the room. He made me so angry. To think I expected him to change after my father's death.

Mom was beside me. Her face looked as though someone had spread red blusher all over it. "Don't you ever talk to your grandfather like that again. He's an old man. He doesn't realize how he sounds."

I lowered my eyes, brushing the hair out of my face. It was an excuse. I didn't want her to see me cry.

"I'm sorry, Mom. I just don't understand why Grandpa always talks to us like that. Doesn't he care about anybody or anything?"

"He wasn't always like that. I think he changed after your father died. He loved his son. He loved God. You see, some people turn bitter when someone they love dies. Sometimes their faith suffers because of the loss."

"He shouldn't treat us like that. I loved Daddy, too."

"I know you did, dear. Grandpa is old, so try to be nice to him and try to understand."

I tried for a brief moment to understand, to put myself in Grandpa's place. I could not understand why he did not open his eyes and see that he had a granddaughter. One who needed his love. Maybe the gift I made for him would show him just how much I cared.

Loud footsteps made me look up. Grandpa was walking toward us. He handed me the present I gave him, then something clicked in my mind. I remember when he used to open gifts from Dad and how happy he was then.

"Here, I'm going to finish my puzzle. You keep the gift," he said, walking away.

I knew in that instant that I had to get through to him. I asked myself: What would my father do at a time like this?

Before he could sit down again, I hurried over where he stood, grabbed his arm and flung the present at him. "Wait, Grandpa! You're going to have a birthday if you like it or not."

"Oh!" Grandpa said, narrowing his eyes. "I suppose you're gonna stop me. What are you now, thirteen?"

"Yes, I am."

Grandpa turned to Mom. "Just listen to her. She sounds just like her father. You ought to do something about her."

I saw the twinkle in Mom's eyes. "Just let her be. I think Cindy is right, open your present."

For a moment Grandpa was too surprised to speak. Then he recovered himself. "Oh, all right. I'll open it then I'm doing my puzzle. Do you hear me, girl?"

"I hear," I said, afraid he would change his mind if I as much as moved one finger.

I watched as he tore off the green wrapping paper and opened the box. "Why, it looks like a puzzle book!"

"Yes," I said. "It is. Do you like it?"

Grandpa looked at me in the oddest way. "This is the kind of puzzle book I've always wanted."

"Cindy made it herself; she printed it out on her computer," Mom told him.

"You made this on your computer?" Grandpa asked me, a frown wrinkling his brow.

I could see a tear form in the corner of his eye. At first I thought I had imagined it, he was actually crying.

"Why, your dad used to make things with his hands, too, when he was about your age. He didn't have a computer, but he was smart."

"You loved him a lot, didn't you, Grandpa?"

Then Grandpa did the strangest thing. I thought he liked my gift. He took the puzzle book and pressed it into my hands; then he turned his back from us. I should have guessed he would act like that.

"You were wrong, girl. I'm going to finish my puzzle," he said, sitting back in his rocker. Then after a long sigh, he took the puzzle book out of my hands.

The words seemed to come out of nowhere. "What are you standing there for? Grab that other chair and get over here. Your puzzle book can't wait all day, you know."

I guess I looked like someone who swallowed a bug. My Grandpa had invited me to work a puzzle from the book I gave him.

"Why?" I asked.

"I'm not sure, girl." He was fighting it. "Maybe because you remind me of your father. Just don't get the idea that you're gonna do puzzles with me every time you visit, cause you ain't."

"It's too bad you never noticed how much I remind you of Dad before this," I told him, sitting in the chair next to him.

"Yep, too bad," he said, grumbling. "We have puzzle work to do. Besides, I want to see how hard these puzzles are in your book."

I wondered if he was putting me on all this time.

I think I am starting to understand Grandpa. He doesn't want to feel pain the way he once did when Dad died. He's afraid to love again or show his feelings. But, we have worked quite a few puzzles since then. I suppose he had to get used to me. I think he's coming around, though. Why the other day when I was sick in bed with the flu, he sent me a gift: a new crossword dictionary. Now, coming from Grandpa, that's a real beginning.

Life In Its Simplicity

Life is the sound of a child's laugh
as the rain tickles his nose.
It is the sight of a flower
stretching its neck to meet the sun,
then shyly folds when the wind
caresses its slender arms.
Life is "the music of the night,"
a clump of dirt waiting for
the first sprinkle of seeds
to fill its empty hole.
It's the wrinkled man or woman
comforting the young, and the young
spilling their blood for country
with a belief that spans all time.
Life is our five senses:
> to smell the sweat of workers;
> hear the cries of children;
> see the purple mountains' crest;
> taste the forbidden fruit and learn
> that touching a rough stone
> will only make us bleed.
> Feeling is all that we are…

We know our lives are like fertile seeds
representing the energy of soul.

Wedding Day Farewell
(1940)

She pressed the roses to her lips,
veined with secrets she held
like the wind at her throat.
Their red dripped a slim vine
of green over white moire
where seed pearls threaded satin
on his body at her feet.

He loved her…to the marrow of her bones,
to the innermost corner of her being…
to her very heart…He loved her.

Remembering the clink of glasses,
the laughter, the rhythmic clapping
of hands, the firey wine,
the mythical spirit of midsummer night,
the inevitable disaffection of death—
she knew dreams die hard.

Home Sickness

Mrs. Jackson stood straining
to see into the conference room
where Dr. Skip talked check-ups.
She remembered earlier times
when aches and pains grew thin
like her skin, and the subtle
changing pulses would beat
against her unprotected heart.
But the cause is more than
medical, more emotional
inside each hidden artery
still waiting to be seen.

When we think of others, our hearts and minds open, and we can feel our self-confidence and the courage we need to help those less fortunate realize they are not alone.

Where Is It, Where Is It?

"What do you suppose we'll eat today?" Martha asked, sitting at the corner table in the Chandler Hall dining room with her hands busily folding and refolding her napkin, legs crossing and uncrossing.

"Last week was animal week," another resident reminded her.

"Oh, yes, that's right, I remember. They gave us little cupcakes shaped like animals. Mine was a green frog with black candied eyes, and Mary Beth wouldn't eat her chocolate dog because she thought it was going to bite her. Imagine that!"

"That's right, Martha," one of the aides told her. "Would you like to help me pass out the juice?"

"I'll help you pass out the juice if you help me find my purse."

"Oh, is it missing?" the aide asked.

"Yes! So are my gold earrings, my red sweater, and my favorite book."

This happened every day. Martha's early Alzheimer's symptoms did not hinder her ability in helping the aides set tables and other small duties. Her outlook was good; her sense of humor and disposition were her outstanding qualities. Ironically, she would complain to the staff that someone was stealing her things, which often happened from time to time when one of the residents would walk the halls in the evening, stop and admire someone's stuffed animal or flower and take it back to their own room. The items often were returned because the name of the person was written on them. But, in the case of Martha, nothing she reported was ever returned because none of the items existed.

A Home Is Not Always Where The Heart Is

Steve is Not John, Or Is He
(an aide feeds me)

This man is not my husband,
the dark eyes are heavy and knowing,
yet gentle and wise.
In memory of John's death,
I hold his love up to the light
so I can see his sacred strings
he ties around my heart.
They are strong like he was,
yet old and worn like me.
Beyond my small powers of observation,
this man, Steve, feeds me food
I no longer want to eat.
His hands help guide
the spoon into my mouth,
sweet than bitter to the taste.
He is firm even when
I pull at his shirt
to wipe my wrinkled hands.
This man is not my husband,
the smile is engaging and strong,
yet tight-lipped and weak like me.
In memory of his life
I press his picture to my breast
so I can feel which one is real:
      Steve or John
They both know me so well!

Mom II
(daughter speaks)

In just a few short months Mom has gotten worse. She refuses to use the bathroom and eats very little. Her agitation and anxiety have gotten out of hand, and trying to help her dress now takes three aides instead of one.

Alzheimer's is, indeed, a sad sight to see; when someone we love deteriorates to such a degree, that nothing medically or physically can stop its progression.

Just the other day when I had to take her to my urologist, she screamed bloody murder and tried desperately to run away. The poor doctor who tried to examine her could not at first because of her behavior, which became intolerable for everyone involved. But, the minute she was back in the nursing home and sitting at the dining room table eating, she became calmer. Almost as if she never knew she had been outside the Home and at a doctor's office.

The only thing that can be done to keep a patient comfortable is medication, which soothes their nerves and lessens their anxious moments, and even seems to help them eat better, but only for a short time. The disease progresses at different rates for different people, but when it reaches the later stages—that is when the time they have left should be well spent with family and friends.

Truthfully, it is very difficult visiting her and to see her go downhill, but in my heart I know it is something I must do—this is when she needs me the most.

Stage Three

My good-bye was casual—no extra
hug or kiss of sentiment
which represents love in its
fondest mode, could bring you back.

No irresponsible trumpet's blare
could herald the moment
more important than you
in each sweeping note.
This contradiction is stifling
like the room. The cause
still shallow with every prayer.
God, I miss you
and your caring ways
as I watch the stars
this darkest night.
Hear the sound of distant
ships sail on foggy silence,
and I think...I see you
under a full moon. Wonder:
Does brain-death ever hurt
when it, too, cries lonely?

You don't understand.

We can only improve what others think of us by improving what we believe, then stand by our convictions.

A Home Is Not Always Where The Heart Is

Mrs. Jackson's Journal Entry
July 1, 2001

It was really strange. Normally, when I feel sorry for myself, I sulk. But this time I was getting angry.

Over and over the meeting raced around in my head and what took place: papers being signed and talking about me as though I wasn't there. I didn't know if I liked this new feeling because I never had the family place me in a nursing home before.

Sometimes I wander too much, because without thinking clearly, I walked into a broom closet at the end of the hall, then shook myself out of my stupor and went, head down, across the hall and into my room where I felt safe and away from all those dark cubbyholes.

Just as I was about to get comfortable in one of the chairs, my daughter walked into the room. She's a fashion designer for a local boutique. I couldn't help but notice the new outfit she wore. Everyone says we look alike. Her hair is a shade darker than mine—a reddish brown to be exact.

She came over to me and placed an arm around my shoulder. "How you doing?" she asked.

"I suppose I could be better."

"Now, Mom, I know how you feel, but this is the best place for you right now. Trust me."

Trust her! I didn't feel like arguing, so I changed the subject. "I'm hungry. Go see what they are having for lunch?" I needed time to calm down.

"Sure, I'll be right back."

I tried to smile, but my lips were stuck. None of them will understand how we really feel.

I got stiffly to my feet, grabbed my sweater and tried to slip out of the room, but not before I heard my daughter call out, "I'll get Mom."

A Home Is Not Always Where The Heart Is

It was becoming a habit—everyone bothering me about something. Just because my memory plays tricks on me, doesn't mean I forget things. Lordy sakes! It happens to all of us when we get older.

The odor of baked chicken filled the dining room when we entered, and watching my daughter talking with the helpers, you'd think they were best friends. At least a couple of my new acquaintances were waiting for me to join them. I call them my prison buddies.

I know it will take time to settle in, but I wonder more if I would ever forgive my family for putting me here. It isn't easy. Now, let me see, what is the name of the movie we are supposed to see tonight?

A Home Is Not Always Where The Heart Is

The Ghost of Uncle Jim

It is the voice
in the bathroom
I hear when duty calls.
The stillness inside
is silent, the wind outside,
a soothing balm to those
who believe and those
who want to believe…I think.

It is the voice
of my Uncle Jim
who once trained dogs
and worked in the mill.
He tells me I need not fear
the coming days here
in the nursing home.
It could be worse…I suppose.

I thank him for visiting,
but I'm tired now, I need my rest.
Do come back another day
when I am wide awake,
not emptying last night's meal.
A girl's gotta get her beauty rest,
                I guess.

Visiting Isn't So Bad

When my brother and I walked into the activity room, we saw Mom sitting with her good friend, Ruth, chatting about their aches and pains. The look on Mom's face when Mike sat next to her was one of puzzlement. It was clear she did not recognize him. This was why he rarely visited the Home. It bothered him to see how much she had changed in just a few short months.

I asked her if she knew him as I slipped next to her; but all she did was stare.

Mike leaned over and kissed her cheek. "Hello, Mom. I missed you."

Tony the aide spotted us sitting with Mom and quickly came over to our table. Leaning over Mike, he said, "You're famous. Everyone knows who you are because your mom always asks for you."

"She does!" Mike asked, surprised.

"Why, she even calls me Mike," Tony said, laughing. "Glad we got to finally meet you."

Then two assistants waved from the other side of the room. "So, this is Mike," one of them called out.

I could see how much this affected him. Taking his hand, I said, "Come on, I'll take you to see Mom's room."

The first thing we showed Mike when he entered the door to her room was Mom's bulletin board filled with family photos, including a photo of Mike's dog, Rocco.

"These are great pictures, Mom," Mike told her. "My favorite is this one of Dad," he said, pointing to it. I could see tears glisten on his cheek in the dim light. "You remember Dad, don't you?" He asked her.

She sat on her bed and pressed her hand on Mike's arm trying to focus on the photo. The small light in her eyes told him all he needed to know. She remembered.

Even though it was difficult for Mike, his love for Mom was stronger than ever. It broke his heart to see her deteriorate, and knowing about her moments she had in dreamlike states that caused her to lose control of her bladder, made it even more difficult for him. I think he believed, at first, that Mom was gone, and that some stranger had taken her place. But I knew in my heart he would come around, because the support group he met with once a week seemed to help him understand her condition better than before.

I know it will take time for him, and that he would visit again. A little knowledge, and the realization that we all age are the biggest hurdles he must take before he can finally say, I understand. His love will see him through—this I have no doubt—and it will help guide him in knowing her better no matter how much she regresses.

Castaways

They bend their snowy crowns
like silver-laced sea birds,
searching for Shangri-la.
Half hitched to worn wings
their Ostrich-like necks
carry the weight of years
with every stooped step they take.
Age has no colored stones
to cast at gray or crashing waves
to wash their rusty plumes;
but flows upward with the wind
and clouds whatever sun sets
on feebleminded night…and we,
proud peacocks preen like gods,
forget that we, too, will search
for the "Fountain of Youth"
when we feel the wind's wrath
rage with the rising tide.

For now, we watch
these flightless birds fly—
to wherever their wings take them.

Fair Game, No Gain

B4 is the winning number.
How can I leave the room a winner
without a good-luck charm to share
so they can win the same as I,
if given half a chance or more.
Flora places worn-out dog head
next to twenty cards. No win in sight.
Funny Fred creeps between the tables.
Tiny Tina waves him down the way.

Some of these players I do not know
in other rooms, filled with other games.
Until they learn the rules and why
they cluster here,
play fair and don't complain or else—
lest they shatter hopes and wins.
This ain't fun…this BINGO!

A Home Is Not Always Where The Heart Is

Rhinestones Are A Girl's Best Friend
(or are they?)

Martha's mouth was set against losing.
She dressed to the nines
every Thursday afternoon for Bingo.
Living in a nursing home, plain clothes
needed added glitter for gaming.
Her days were filled with choosing
bracelets, earrings, and rhinestones,
outshining all the rest:
White-framed picture hat,
an orange scarf for added color,
and a pair of brown sandals.
Her wardrobe set for a win
from another era, another time.
Martha dressed for bingo and for love.

Frank helped in the activity room,
counting cards and fruit punch,
oblivious to Martha and her hat.
He only knew some silly old woman
played games on Thursdays in jewels.

Martha purple-dabbed the cards—
her determination as strong
as his opposing different views.
Until another Thursday, she will try again
to open doors his eyes may never see.

The more smiles we have, the more wrinkles we get: Our lifelines

A Home Is Not Always Where The Heart Is

Who Says You Shouldn't Smoke

Sitting quietly by the window and using his inhaler for his emphysema, Dan would often reminisce with visitors about his army stint during World War II. He would recall his days in France when German prisoners huddled in the shadowy and quiet room in the compound where he was stationed. How they would sit with their heads pressed against the walls with no fear in their eyes.

Dan was a Sergeant who believed in fairness with a sense of honor, and because of that, the prisoners were treated with respect. They, at times, joked and teased one another, dispelling the belief that all German soldiers during the war were hostile towards Americans. At least in Dan's quarters anyway.

One day Dan was making the rounds checking that everything was secure, when he noticed one of the prisoners stretched out on the floor holding a pencil and sketching a woman's face. Impressed with what he saw, Dan immediately instructed an interpreter to relate to the German that he would make a deal with him. He told the prisoner that he would give him two packs of cigarettes—along with the supplies he needed—if he would paint a picture of his wife from a wallet-sized photograph he carried in his pocket. Cigarettes were hard to come by for prisoners, and this particular German was delighted to make the exchange.

It took two weeks to finish, and what resulted was a beautifully painted portrait of Dan's wife that looked exactly the way he remembered her: dark chestnut hair, dark brown eyes, ruby lips, and the string of iridescent pearls complemented the lavender sweater she wore in the small photo. The likeness was remarkable. He could not praise the prisoner enough for work well done. This, he decided, would be her Valentine's gift when he returned home.

Opening his eyes in his room at the nursing home, trying to catch his breath, and not sure whether it was his disease or the memory of his dead wife that brought on the new constriction in his lungs, he managed to stand up. A smile tugged the corners of his lips as he turned his head to stare at the portrait that hung above his bed. Picking up his inhaler and turning it over in his hand, he said, "If I could do it all over again, I wouldn't change a thing. It was worth seeing her face when I got home—and all because of two packs of cigarettes."

A Home Is Not Always Where The Heart Is

Love Letter To My Wife
(1944)

My dearest wife of five years,
I sit in camp with the boys
under a water-dry September sun
and think of you and your garden.
How you rouse a flock of butterflies
with just a gentle touch.

At night—
creatures of the air weave
a crystal cloak around you
in the shining silver shadows.

In day—
I miss your sparkling eyes
and sunburned summer skin.
Habit being so strong, dear love,
I send a kiss in every word,
and pray the sweeping wind will carry
more than heart-filled love your way.

For now—
fear not this plight of war;
our separation a temporary parting.
The boys of autumn know
my every deed and time well spent
keeps idle hands still busy,
as I count each day, each hour.

A Home Is Not Always Where The Heart Is

Till then—
tend your flower garden,
water those dried-perched vines,
and when they grow to highest hill,
I'll be home.

It won't be long when our empty arms
are filled with more than memories.

        Love, Dan

If we look under a microscope at ourselves, we see all the little things we've done become larger than life.

An Aide In Need

Vickie passed away a few days ago. Ellen, her favorite aide, sat at the social worker's desk wiping her eyes as she said, "She was such a sweet lady. Her losing weight and loss of hearing never stopped her from visiting the other residents. I will miss her."

Jeannine leaned against the wall, nodding her head as she listened to Ellen remember Vickie. "We used to go to all the funerals, but after a while, we stopped because it is impossible attending them all anymore." No wonder these aides were discouraged at times; they witnessed many who never had visitors, or witnessed some of the family members who would start out visiting, then gradually stayed away.

Tony, too, says it can get a person down, and yet it is very rewarding helping those who need it most. He remembers working in a Home that would feed its residents sandwiches every day. On special occasions, they would get meat, vegetables, and potato. He believes this has now changed.

Annette loves the activities *Spirit Care Home* schedules monthly: Bingo; film festivals; exercise day; crafts; coffee hour; dog and cat day; picnics; field trips. "Seeing the joy on their faces when they partake in these activities—especially in their eyes—and knowing they are still able to do them, is rewarding."

Judy laughs at some of the antics that go on during cleaning day. Every Saturday a few of the residents get verbal. They hate to be disrupted from their daily routines. "And shower day! You get an education in cuss words—that is for sure. Many older people hate to take showers."

Rosetta says she tries to be strong, but when she goes home all the tension comes out by relaxing in her pool, floating on her back and letting the sun warm her skin. "I think a good hug for some of the residents helps me get through some of the more stressful days.

Ben makes sure he visits Fay, one of his favorites. He loves to hear her sing. "She'll sit by the bird cage and talk to the birds, and doesn't seem to mind that they don't talk back to her. Then she will start singing, and before you know it, every person around will join in 'You are my sunshine.'"

Rhonda in admitting (a senior citizen herself) says: "I wish I would have known about places like *Spirit Care Home* twenty years ago when my mother stayed with me before she died. It would have been so much easier for me as well as for her."

Alice, one of the nurses, sums it up best when she says: "I look at it this way: we all are going to get old, and if there are places like *Spirit Care Home* around when and if we need them, it makes things a bit easier knowing there are people who care."

A Home Is Not Always Where The Heart Is

Father Hangs In Chandler Hall
(Akeia, a long-time aide)

The residents admired my painting
of the ancient nature trails.
The palette sported dazzling pigments
as if they twirled in a coil of water,
cascading down the river's back.
It was only my first dabble
through time's wasteland echoes,
and each brush stroke made me strong,
but not brave enough to place
the painting next to my father's grave,
so it hangs on the wall.

He used to walk through the foliage
that formed an emerald temple
where heavy air cracked, and a gust
of wind wrung the crowns
of the trees like broken feathers,
shattering the stone in his palm
he carried for luck.
But it ran out, and his spirit that lived
with mine in the river
is embedded in the painting…still.

Nurse Katherine On Dementia

Not only does one lose their memory in stages, one loses their way of life, many times their dignity, and their sociable attitudes.

In the later stages it breathes, smothers, kills, dies, brings dark dreams, goes beyond the norm, then reaches deep inside the mind pulling pieces of reality and digesting it until one feels as though the top of their head were blown to pieces.

Depending on the patient, I have seen some who needed medication to help ease their anxieties, their feelings of loss, and their will to live. Of course, some do not get violent, but many do, and it is at these times we must care for them and make them as comfortable as possible.

Vigil

Mother rests on chalk-white bed
groping at tubes where humming sounds
vibrate the shadowed-silent room.
Tears glisten under moonlit window
where I stand in quiet prayer.
I do not ask for living life,
but death to claim her soul.
To take her to the light of God
where angels wrap their wings in white.

My eyes search far and wide
where stars are sprinkled in crystal night
for signs to ease her way
and hands to guide her through.
I know her spirit is ready to soar
like the fledgling from its nest.
Her new home waits in greening fields—
in shades of vivid-flowered pots
where gathered family and friends abide.

Mother rests on chalk-white bed,
no longer groping at tubes.
She is, at last, in her heavenly home:
a speck of light in the darkness.

A Home Is Not Always Where The Heart Is

Randy Stuffing His Face

Throughout our lives we must take time to record all our lessons, then later sit down and enjoy the play back.

Mother Said There Would Be Days Like This

Gladys constantly frets about her mother, imagining she is still home caring for the children or in the hospital giving birth to another sister or brother. Even though her mother has been dead for more than thirty years, Gladys' mind and heart—like so many others—aches for earlier times where she felt more comfortable and safe from the outside world. In missing her mother she has, at the same time, regressed to that child she once was, but only in her mind.

Some miss their premarital days when they lived with their parents, while others dwell on their immediate family and friends. But Gladys cannot help her insecurity; her mouse-like teeth widen as she speaks the words "Did my mother call me today?" Her mind will not rest until she hears that everything is fine at home and that her mother will call soon, or has already. Just simple reassurance can soothe most of the more agitated residents, because trying to explain why a mother or father or another family member they miss is unable to visit them, or the real reason why, can often do more harm than good. Especially if the person is high strung, or cannot grasp what another person is trying to tell them. Then there are those where reality is a must to help them strengthen their minds and put a sparkle back into their eyes. Again, it depends on the person and their situation.

The phone rings in the dining room, Gladys carefully listens to see if her mother is asking about her. Jane, the nurse, smiles, tells Gladys all is fine. Gladys picks up her spoon, licks her lips, smiles. Yes, all is fine, until the next phone call.

A Home Is Not Always Where The Heart Is

Few Visitors, Fewer Friends

Once the pale light of the moon
broke through our curtain of darkness,
and foothills gathered stars,
we knew nothing would change,
not even our lives
that drifted through days and weeks
in a house angled to catch
the first drops of rain before the storm.
Powerless to fight the reality of things,
we lived our memories through dreams.
And sometimes we'd see the tear-streaked roof
leak its way through awkward moments—
where belief is a stranger
and truth is never seen at all.

We are guilty if we stay cooped up here
without the sun to warm us,
or feel the earth on our tender skin
because our doors are locked and our windows
barred from all that we were.

Someday, years from now, most of us
will see death as a friend because
some of us will still be remembered.

To gain spiritual wisdom, follow the river as it flows through hardest rocks and darkest night, then swim up hill to hear the silence speak to you.

A Home Is Not Always Where The Heart Is

Mrs. Jackson's Journal Entry
(August 23, 2001)

I could tell that Loretta enjoyed being a nurse, except when she had to attend to the cleaning and replacing of a pessary, and most especially when the patient refused to cooperate. Like the day Agnes had to have hers cleaned, Loretta knew it wasn't going to be easy. It never was with Agnes, who only thought of Loretta as the cleaning lady.

And what a day it was for Agnes. She spotted Loretta and three aides coming around the corner. But before Loretta and the aides could reach the door, Agnes darted past them as fast as her legs could carry her, which wasn't very fast and headed down the hall.

"Help! They're coming to invade my private parts again!" Agnes yelled at the top of her lungs.

All eyes turned to the door as Agnes backed into the smallest dining room where I was trying to eat my lunch in the east section of the Home. Flying trays and chairs missed several seniors sitting at tables, and two residents' dogs raced into the kitchen nearly knocking Maggie, the dietitian, off her feet. (We are allowed to have our animals visit once a week.)

My word, it was a mess. The silly woman certainly knows how to disrupt our peaceful eating room.

She grabbed my sleeve yelling, "Save me, save me!"

"From what?" I said trying to pull my arm away.

"From them," Agnes pointed at the door as she crawled under the nearest table and slid over next to the wall. "I'm not a baby. I don't need changing."

I saw Loretta enter the room, walk over to our table, and bend down to extend her hand to help Agnes stand up. "Come on out, it's time to eat. We'll attend to your needs later."

Loretta knew eating would settle Agnes down because it was her favorite thing to do at the Home. In fact, it was almost like a sedative whenever she became agitated or frightened, and right about then I would have liked to stuff her mouth with more than food.

Agnes finally came out from under the table and sat next to me. "I see you came to your senses," I told her.

Leaning over my tray Agnes whispered into my ear, "I'm not so dumb, you know. I'll just tell them I'm tired after I eat. They'll forget all about me."

I couldn't hold my laughter any longer. I knew Loretta would eventually clean the pessary, and everything would go back to normal. But trying to talk to someone in Agnes' state of mind was like asking Dr. Skip to let me go home.

"Enjoy your meal, Agnes, I'll see you later," Loretta said winking at me as she left the room.

"You can bet you'll see her later," I told Agnes. "I mean it isn't every day a girl gets caught in open season."

I must admit this place is getting more interesting the more I stay here. I can't wait for Bingo day; maybe I'll finally win a pot or two.

Note: Pessary holds a protruding bladder.

Day In And Day Out
(on admitting a new resident)

Scanning the empty corridor
we can almost picture an array
of pastel lab coats coloring
the cobwebbed corner; phantom ghosts
grouped around the desk
fill the narrow hallway. Their eyes
alighting on a young aide's form
pleading time-spent youth once more.

A glimmer of hope casts a sliver of light
across the rose-patterned room
where residents bide their time.
The sound of footsteps echoes through walls
as we march in lifeless lines.
Our caretakers reappear in real-time
all dressed to fit the ceremony.

A Home Is Not Always Where The Heart Is

Safe From The Outside World

Leave the door locked, lose the key
as the morning light warms us inside.
Listen
the wind song soon takes wings
and dances against the window.
Gushing torrents of rain rinse away
yesterday's muddy residue;
glistening drops pearled on leaves
softens our daydreams.

Leave the window locked, keep us safe
wrapped in our own security.
Feel it
the sunshine soon takes heart
and warms our troubled souls.
Sun and rain and wind, our Home
safe and warm…ours!

A Home Is Not Always Where The Heart Is

Once More In Winter

As I stand by the window
I see children ice skating
across the frozen pond,
I hear broken tree limbs snap,
pointing fingers at rooftops
where packed snow sits
like stiff doilies against
the silver backcloth of sky.
I smile watching a sparrow
resting on eaves of ice,
anticipating its thaw.

Darkness calls and I know
my time has come to rest.
Age has slipped its arm
around me to keep me warm.
But in dreams I shake it off
and grasp the icy fingers
of winter's brisk wind, let it
caress me like it did in youth.
It is all I have left. It is all I want:
My time, my only time to skate.

A Home Is Not Always Where The Heart Is

Mom in her sweater

Never hesitate to tell someone you love them; you may never get another chance to remember.

A Home Is Not Always Where The Heart Is

Andrew Sees The Light

I don't often tell people about my experiences or stories, but I will this time because I need to get it out in the open before I die.

About ten years ago one of my daughter's friends surprised me. She handed me an envelope and insisted I look at its contents. So, of course, I opened the envelope, and to my utter amazement, there was a photograph of a young woman dressed in a pale blue and white robe, like they wore in biblical times. A veil draped over her head, and she seemed to be suspended above the trees with her arms extended, and a rosary hung from each of her hands. At first I thought I was looking at a double exposure. I found out later that the photo was taken in Madjugorje, Yugoslavia.

The feeling that hit me after viewing the photograph was one I shall never forget. It didn't happen right then. It happened after I left my daughter's house with the picture in my wallet: I almost had an accident. I became dizzy, incoherent, and felt as though I was floating above the ground as I stepped out of the car. The scenery around me was such a vivid green, and the sun was so bright, I could look directly at it without hurting my eyes.

After I walked into the house I burst into tears and felt such an elation of love that I had never experienced in my life. It took me two days to get back to normal.

My wife and daughter worried about me. I can't explain myself, or what happened. Ever since that day I see visions. Some call me psychic. Some call me crazy.

I think I know how some of those television psychics feel, or how the great poets and philosophers felt when they walked the woods in search of truth.

Now, I'm not trying to get anyone into religion or whatever you want to call it. I just thought I'd get it off my chest. It is an unforgettable and enlightening experience, and I often wondered if something is going on. Is there a message?

A Home Is Not Always Where The Heart Is

Today, I sit here in the Home and see things, images, and can oftentimes predict the future. Being an old man makes it even harder convincing anyone what I see as real. That's all right. When my time comes I'll be ready because I know there is a place for all of us on the other side of the light.

Right Temporal Lobe
(is located above the right ear where the psychic is housed)

You sit and stare with eyes focused
on things we do not see.
A small light frames your face.
It is almost as if you have a gift
to look inside the face of heaven.
You hold a tidal wave of emotions
inside yourself, needing release.
What you see through the window,
in your mind, delights us, frightens us,
tells us we all have windows,
and getting on the other side is inevitable.
You tell us you almost feel as though
you are sitting with God on his front porch
appreciating the tree of life.
There is a sadness when each leaf falls,
but it is universal truth, for life and death
are one. You say new leaves grow back
in the spiritual roundness of the whole—
a star-crossed light is born.

A Home Is Not Always Where The Heart Is

It's All In The Heart

Some residents are given medications to ease their anxieties, while others have therapy. But in the case of Violet, the only thing that seemed to appease her was listening to the song, "Achy Breaky Heart."

About nine years before she developed Alzheimer's disease, she loved to go to the country music dance clubs, and whenever that song was played on the jukebox, Violet would get up out of her chair and dance.

Music was an everyday occurrence during eating hours at the home, and every once in a while some of the residents would sing. Last week, after Violet's daughter instructed one of the aides to play Achy Breaky on the overhead speakers in the dining room, Violet decided to try dancing in the corner. That wouldn't, ordinarily, be a problem, but being that Violet was in a wheelchair, she got carried away and broke her leg.

The Home decided—in keeping with her best interest—not to play the song anymore during leisure time, which later caused Violet to become depressed. She stopped eating and refused to communicate. Not even her dog, Goldie, could lift her spirits. Until one day one of the new aides, Tony, came up with an idea. He wheeled Violet into the dining room, placed a security pad across the front of her wheelchair to keep her from standing up then turned on the CD player. Not caring if she was restrained or not, she kept her eyes shut. Until a few minutes later she opened them in disbelief. "Achy Breaky Heart" burst out of the speakers.

What she saw was Tony dancing and sliding across the room. The staff and residents were singing and clapping to the song. Violet was so happy, she could hardly contain herself from wiggling and pushing against the pad as the music filled the room. (Because of Tony the Home now plays the song daily and makes sure Violet's security pad is hooked to the front of her wheelchair.)

At night when the lights are turned down and everyone is sleeping, Violet is still awake in her bed, close to the dining room, listening for

Tony and her favorite song. What she hears, instead, are other sleepless residents searching for others' songs in other rooms.

We Watch, We Wonder, We Wait No More

They see us lurking,
perched like sentinels
outside their corner desks.
Our probing eyes
watch their every move.
We hear the sound of voices
invade our quiet time.
    Time to eat.
    Time to take a bath.
    Time to exercise.
    Time to go to bed.
Someone should have told them
seniors are sometimes fragile,
we need our separate space.

New lists to fill:
    Pills crushed in cups.
    Depends our last resort.
    Wheelchairs crowd corridors
signifies our change of life
here in this Home of homes.

Our lives are young seeds that flower and blossom in spring then whither and die in winter, until another spring when gentle rain brings forth new flowers from newer seeds.

An Apple A Day

You never would have guessed that Christine, a short, silver haired woman, once was a head nurse at a local hospital; that she volunteered her time by reading stories to children at a day care center just eight years ago. Today she sits quietly with the other patients waiting for her lunch to arrive.

What caused her to be a resident at the Home was noticeable difficulty in performing her tasks. She often got lost and eventually forgot where she lived. Her family had no choice but to admit her as a patient at *Spirit Care Home* in Chandler Hall: the Alzheimer section for those with early symptoms of the disease.

When talking to her no real sentences come out of her mouth, only a few muddled words. Her outlook is good, and she interacts well with the newer residents by patting them on their backs. Her nature is extremely uplifting, yet at the same time, one of concern for herself, and knowing she cannot express her feelings, will often frustrate her. But through it all, Christine will often bond with the staff members, perhaps due to her training in nursing.

All the nurses, aides, and doctors strive to maintain their communicative skills with the patients instead of a too authoritative demeanor, which can sometimes intimidate many of them by being uncooperative in return.

The head nurse just recently mentioned that Christine should be transferred to the medicare section in the near future. Her Alzheimer symptoms are slowly progressing to the middle stages.

Over Developed
(the other side of youth)

My mind clouds like film
from over exposure.
When it clears pictures
race in technicolor clips
like watered-down reflections.

Drifting in and out of sleep
I steal sacred hours
to reassess my life.
On learning, I draw a map
at heartache's cost, wait
to follow directions
where interference reigns.
It takes time, and time
is all I have—

Yet, my egg-shell existence
cracks at the seams, the map
shreds pieces from the whole,
old age intervenes the crossing.

A Home Is Not Always Where The Heart Is

It's A Matter of Time

Lillie, in her red cardigan,
stuffs her pockets with old coins
she finds from older times.

Frank plays checkers with Tim,
jumping across the board
in red and black annoyance.

Stella, in her purple pantsuit,
closes then reopens bathroom door
not sure if she should go.

Allen switches TV stations
searching for Loretta Young
caught in channels time has lost.

Ethel, in her white winter shawl,
sits idle like the clock on the wall,
a mortal enemy till the end.

For those who find that time is short
will form a line around them.

A Home Is Not Always Where The Heart Is

Frank and Tim playing checkers

"How many angels can stand on the point of a needle?"
More than you can imagine, or see.

Mrs. Jackson's Journal Entry
October 14, 2001

I made sure I was the first one up, which is rare for me. Then I selected what I thought a smart oldie would wear to breakfast: gray stretch pants and a bright yellow pullover sweater with my name on it. It gives me an identity instead of being one of the crowd.

"What are you doing up so early? You sick or something?" Agnes asked me when she entered the dining room carrying her baby doll.

"Nah! I'm hungry, that's all" I told her.

Agnes studied me for a few minutes before she dropped into her favorite chair, the one facing the door, then noiselessly plopped her doll on the table. With a steady hand she lifted the doll's dress up and slipped her finger inside the diaper. She was obviously distressed when she said, "My baby needs changing. She's wet."

I wanted to tell her that naturally her baby doll was wet; she laid it on the spilled milk next to her bowl. "You can change her later," I told her, "I'm trying to eat."

Munching on my toast, I studied the doll, trying to look interested. It was neatly wrapped with white strips of cloth; a red heart was on its head; and pink nail polish was painted on its toes. Quite sloppy I must add. I figured if it made Agnes happy having a baby doll, so be it. As long as I didn't have to hold it or change its diapers, I'd be fine.

To change the subject, I asked her if she liked my new sweater with my name on it.

By the look on her face, I thought she was impressed. But then she quickly changed her expression to disbelief. "Today's not Sunday," she said, pointing to my clothes. "You're too dressed up for breakfast."

"Who said it was Sunday?" I raised my voice. "Smart seniors always dress like this."

"Smart seniors! Who are you kidding? I think I'm going to be sick," Agnes said, clutching her stomach.

I wasn't sure if it was my flashy sweater or the cereal she ate. She was getting on my nerves. Maybe because I was looking forward to a peaceful morning—her baby-doll mood was the last thing I needed right now. "If I were you, Agnes, I'd get myself out of here before I decide to take your doll's head off."

"Make me," she said, spitting her tongue out, standing behind Julie the aide, for protection.

What an opportunity. I stood up, grabbed the spoon off the table and waved it in her face. "Why don't you shut up and eat," I said.

She snatched the spoon out of my hand so fast, that it barely missed Julie's head. After she made sure I wasn't going to chase her, she bolted out of the room.

I heard her running in the direction of the nursing station, yelling, "I'm going to tell Dr. Skip on you."

Some oldies can be a pain in the neck, especially Agnes. On my way back to my room, I turned to wave at her. She was standing in the leisure room pressing her doll's face against the glass. I think it's great that she loves her doll, but does she have to let the world know it.

I'm sorry, Agnes," I yelled out to her. "Are you still angry with me?"

Turning from the window, she said: "No, not really. But do you have to wear those bright colors and your name flashing like a neon sign? You look…"

"Smart," I finished for her.

"Well, yeah."

I couldn't hurt her feelings anymore. So, I did the next best thing, even if it almost killed me to do it. "Bring me your baby, Agnes. I'll be happy to change her diaper for you,"

Agnes left the room, still looking at me with a smile playing with the corners of her lips. I smiled back at her as I carried the doll by the leg into her room to change its milk-soaked diaper.

Two Days Later:

I couldn't believe my eyes. Agnes came into my room wearing a green sweater with her name on it. "I still think you are a silly old woman wearing your name all over the place just to get attention," she said. Then she placed her baby doll onto my lap. The doll wore the exact same sweater that Agnes had on, but with my name stitched in bright red letters across the front. Will wonders ever cease?

A Home Is Not Always Where The Heart Is

Hard Facts, Harder Truths

> *O my God, I cry by day,*
> *but you do not answer;*
> *and by night,*
> *but find no rest.*
> 　　　　Psalms 22:1-2

The residents strain against
the front of their wheelchairs
tighter than phlegm-filled throats
holding their breath from the terror
of being found staring through
sun-stained windows and barred
from doors too high to climb.

The residents press heads
against brick walls built hard
like their life penetrating
pores with present and past
not caring whether they live or die
in a world round with wounds
that don't always heal.

The residents resign
still trapped behind walls wrapped
with cellophane clear enough
to read between the lines
these words don't always write.

Bath Wars
(a wet dialogue)

Every Wednesday and Saturday was bath day, and for Loretta and the aides, that meant lots of cussing and water fights. Today was one of those days for Agnes who hated baths more than any other resident in the Home.

"I don't want to take a bath!" Agnes yelled. "I'm clean enough."

"It's time, dear. You don't want to get bugs now, do you?" Loretta asked her as she gently led her towards the bathtub.

"There aren't any bugs in here. You're just trying to scare me," Agnes told her slowly descending into the tub searching the water.

"No, I'm not. It's important to keep clean. We'll use your favorite bubble bath—you know, the one with Princess Leia on the top of the bottle. That should make you feel better."

The reason why most of the residents hated to take baths was because of their thin and sensitive skin. They become chilled easier, and so it was understandable why so many hated them.

"How often do you take a bath?" Agnes asked Loretta, who stood next to the tub dripping water on the bath matt.

"Every day. Actually, I take a shower instead. They're faster and it almost feels like standing out in the rain."

"Like standing in the rain!" Agnes said, bouncing Princess Leia in the water. "Do you think I can dance in the rain?"

That caught Loretta off guard. Then with the biggest smile, she said: "Why yes, Agnes. We can do that, and we could call it your Dancing Rain time. What do you think of that?"

"My own rain dance. I think I'm going to like that. Can Princess Leia dance with me, too?"

Loretta patted her hand and told her, "She certainly can. Now let's finish up here and pour some more bubble bath into your water until then."

A Home Is Not Always Where The Heart Is

Three days later, after taking her first shower at the Home, Agnes came out of the bathroom singing. She actually loved it. But Loretta only shook her head as she followed behind Agnes soaking wet.

"What happened to you," one of the aides asked her, laughing.

"Oh! Agnes and I were dancing in the rain. Guess I got a little wet. Now some of the other residents want to rain dance—take showers instead of baths, that is. Except we have a problem. The only bubble bath we have in stock are Darth Vaders!"

The aide rolled her eyes. "Oh, I can see that now—little Darth Vaders dancing in the rain with the female residents. You thought they hated their bath days before!" It took a while, but finally the patients (most of them) started to enjoy their bath days better, thanks to the family members who donated special shower gels and bath items. And what happened to the Darth Vader bubble baths? They were wrapped by the seniors and given as Christmas gifts for the children in the local hospitals.

Since we are all one, and if we love ourselves, we love the whole world.

Believe II

To love and laugh often
and smile in the face of adversity.
To respect those around you
by going out of your way
to earn the approval of children.
Forgive your enemies
by forgiving yourself.
To face critics with an open mind
and to learn by experience.
Show praise in others
by giving a helping hand.
Appreciate beauty in all things,
for there is beauty in you.
Walk and take time to play
by stopping to smell the flowers.
Sing and rejoice because you have
helped one person believe in God.
You can do all these things because
you have lived...

Mom III
(daughter speaks and teens visit)

Arriving on an early morning visit to see Mom, I passed a group of teenagers standing just inside the front door waiting for their teacher to admit them inside the Home. After she came, they followed me down the hallway leading into the dining room where the residents were eating breakfast.

I noticed a few of the girls stopped at the door and stared at the seniors, almost afraid to approach them. If they expected to see older citizens sitting around the room—happy and enjoying their lives, they were quickly awakened to the reality of nursing homes. What they really saw was a room full of residents: half of them were in wheelchairs unable to talk and being spoon-fed; the other half was a combination of incoherent or alert seniors needing attention.

One of the girls walked slowly up to one of the men sitting against the wall and asked if she could help feed him. Another girl wanted to know how the Home worked; what their daily routines were like; and how many activities were planned for the month.

They seemed to relax more the longer they stayed with the residents. But, truthfully, at times it does become depressing.

Mom sat watching the teens blend in with everyone, and their caring attitudes gave the aides a break until lunchtime when the students had to leave and go back to school.

What goes on at a nursing home (not all) was never clearer than it was that day. Some of the teens' views on their visit were more than honest:

Judy: "I kept thinking how we take them for granted, that some people really don't care about them."

Pam: "Truthfully, seeing those who don't speak anymore really bothered me. I thought…I could be like that."

Darlene: "I kept picturing my mom ending up in a Home, and it frightened me."

Karen: "I was angry. Not at what I saw, rather what I didn't see…more visitors."

Marilyn: "I wanted to give every one of them my heart. It was sad to see them so helpless."

Michelle: "It wasn't easy. But once I got to know a few of them, I think I understood aging better."

Julie: "My favorite of them all was Mrs. Jackson. She had me cracking up, especially when she let me read some of her journal entries. She certainly is colorful."

Jennifer's visit was inspiring: "I sat with Andrew most of the time, and I have to admit I enjoyed his predictions about me. When he told me I would be a nurse, I told him that's exactly what I wanted to be some day. I swear I saw a light coming from his face. It probably was a reflection from the window!"

A Home Is Not Always Where The Heart Is

What Are They Thinking?
(inside and outside the mind of Victoria)

Inside:
A voice sweeps through me
anchored in muscle and bone,
pressed against a battered brain
with distorted memories all jumbled,
and I try to focus on the words
calling out beyond the confusion.
Simple words, really. I remember
baking bread, Joe's cat,
hurrying to school, hurrying home,
anxious, worried, happy, and sad,
a frozen moment watching Phillip
shovel snow, wash windows,
all in the same season. A black and white
dress worn at Tom's funeral, crying.

Outside:
Why is that man cutting the grass now?

Inside:
Rain pounds the sidewalk, Mrs. Calley
crosses my yard, brings cookies in
the church I see Father Brown light
the candle—the wax drips in slow motion
all fire-red in my fireplace. Stockings
hang, a doll's head pops the wrappings—
some sort of holiday! Christmas?

Outside:
I watch him cut more grass.
His arms sweat in checkered shirt.

Inside:
Another face swims in my view.
She bends to feed me—not hungry.
More flashes of earlier days
intermingle these fragments into
thoughts. Like playing marbles
and shooting darts one memory at a time.

The sound of the lawn mower stops.

A Home Is Not Always Where The Heart Is

For Every Tree That Grows

If a siren goes off in a remote area,
is there sound if no one is around to hear it?
The mechanism inside emotes sound waves.
A tree stands before you. If you close
your eyes, will it disappear?
There are natural noises like the tree
that falls in a forest.
There are man-made noises like sirens.
We who live in a Home
are never seen nor heard. Our solace
draws comfort from trees.

A Home Is Not Always Where The Heart Is

Future World—2090
(Alzheimer's cured—Age Continues)

Inside the glass nursing home
wearing their season grays,
they come from their rooms
to search the halls in wonder.
Cold fists jammed at empty air
uncurl like the sound of wind sending
a soft mist through rough waters outside.
To warm them up, hot rum gives them
the spirit to lift arms
and fire strength in the weak.
Living together in shades:
black, white, red, and yellow,
their foreign tongues are wiped clean
from years of strangeness.
In wise words they tell one another:
It is a new world in an old land
where children play untouched,
and are free to shoot hugs instead of drugs
into each other's arms.
Beyond the golden gate,
a revolving door spins a galaxy
of broken wings that once soared
to greater heights before dying
in iron wars with iron lungs
still attached to memories.
Only a shortcut through woods
could lead them back to youth,

A Home Is Not Always Where The Heart Is

back to their old ways of restless wonder.
Still, one weak foot, one strong hand
could crush their last crusade
and force the world to see them
for what they really are……

It's All Relative

So that you reflect on these matters
in solitude, walk proud among
the living and share the moment
with those you love. For there are those
moments you will not be able to cherish
much more than this. Hold fast
your dreams and continue to reflect
on past deeds, both good and bad.
Then trust yourself to love all that you are;
but more than this, love all that you're not,
and just be content with one another.
Listen, learn, and be happy. It's your birthright.

Mrs. Jackson's Journal Entry
(December 10, 2001)

The buzz of the fire drill echoed along the hall. The oldies scrambled out of their rooms wondering what the racket was about, and when Mabelle and I raced to see who would be the first one to reach the exit door, I slammed against someone wearing a brown plaid shirt, knocking him flat on his back. I guess I didn't see him coming; but when I saw his face, the idea of leaving him all crumbled in a heap crossed my mind. Being the good sport that I am, and seeing Dr. Skip so helpless, I gave in and tried to help him up.

"You okay, doc?" I asked him, handing him his stethoscope.

"I guess so. Are you all right, yourself, Mrs. Jackson?"

"I'm fine. I'm sorry if I hurt you."

"You didn't hurt me," he said, straightening his jacket.

Mabelle, who stood behind us, handed me my walker. "Thanks, dear. Looks like the good doc here could use it more than me," I told her.

Dr. Skip rarely laughs, but this time he howled, just like a werewolf. If I looked close enough, I bet I'd see fangs growing inside his mouth.

"Well, doc, you have a good day," I told him as I grabbed Mabelle's arm. "We gotta go."

After we found ourselves outside, Mabelle said, "Dr. Skip is planning a Christmas party for us, and you'll never guess what he came up with to celebrate?"

"Let's see…a giant candy cane, so he can place it above our heads and bop us when we get cranky."

"Nope. He hired a blimp. I mean a man to work the blimp, and he's going to have colored lights and a sign put on the side of it."

I thought I was hearing wrong. "A blimp! Doctors don't use blimps."

A Home Is Not Always Where The Heart Is

We both laughed so hard, we doubled over. I tried to picture Dr. Skip sitting on top of a large yellow blimp holding a huge vacuum cleaner sucking up everybody's money at the Home.

Breaking my spell Mabelle yanked me around the building. A large white sign with green letters and a red bow stood against the wall. "What is that?" I asked her.

"A sign. What did you expect, a billboard for the blimp? Read it, silly."

"Well, in that moment my heart melted. The sign read: "Join us for Fire Works at 9:00 P.M. at Spirit Care Home on December 20th." Because the Home is located on a large piece of land, a sparkler show in winter is no problem, but a blimp! I guess Dr. Skip really cares about us after all. I wonder if his family will attend. I hear his wife plays bingo.

P. S.

Most people know that Dr. Skip is a highly respected doctor. He certainly knows how to send us seniors to nursing homes. I guess I can be a little hard on him at times. He is a good doctor.

Our soul-light shines through our eyes, and sometimes it changes colors, dims, but never goes out. It's eternal like we are and just as bright.

Andrew Sees More Light

"Please, Andrew, tell my future. Will I be able to leave the Home and be with my family again?" Willie asked, sitting on his bed on the other side of the room they shared.

Andrew placed his hands over his eyes and counted to ten. Then he slowly opened them as his face turned a glowing white. "No, you will not go home, Willie. Your back and legs are still too weak, so I believe you will have to make the best of it here."

Now Willie often got frustrated with Andrew because he never predicted what he wanted to hear—that he would go home for good.

"I don't know why I waste my time asking you things. You never tell the truth. I'll be going home for Christmas. So, you are wrong."

Andrew just smiled and nodded his head. "Yes, Willie, my boy, you are going home for Christmas, but only for a visit. You will be back, and remember what else I told you at an earlier reading."

"Oh, that. I'll meet a new woman in my life. Now that one, Andrew, is one of your craziest predictions yet." Or was it?

A week after Christmas Willie returned from his family gathering, and the first thing he told Andrew when he entered their room made Andrew laugh.

"My sister had the nerve to invite an old wallflower for dinner."

"A flower you say?" Andrew asked with a knowing grin.

"You know perfectly well what I'm talking about."

"Tell me about her, Willie?" Andrew already knew.

Willie put his small overnight bag next to his dresser, sat in his corner chair, and removed his shoes.

"Well, she ain't bad lookin'. It's just her darn obsession with exercise. She boasts that she lost 30 pounds by breathing the weight off—some new fangled exercise where you take in lots of air."

"What bothers you more, Willie, your own health or your fear of women?" Andrew asked him.

Two weeks later Andrew stood by the window watering his favorite plant, when out of the corner of his eye he saw Willie walk past the open door on the arm of a woman. Turning his head, he heard Willie say: "Thanks for visiting, Elizabeth. Of course, I love to exercise. Andrew, my roommate, holds my legs while I stretch, and I can even do push ups now by inhaling lots of air."

"Oh, Willie, how wonderful," she said.

Yes, Andrew thought to himself. Willie is inhaling lots of air all right—a lot of hot air.

Willie has relaxed more at the Home since meeting Elizabeth, and Andrew continues to advise him with lots of enlightening revelations.

A Home Is Not Always Where The Heart Is

Emily Recites A Holiday Poem
(first verse found)

The joyful season is here for us all.
We can see it in the trees on corners
and nooks, decked out in ornamentation.
We hear it in the halls and aisles and parking lots.
People call a greeting when they pass by.
We can feel it in the air. It's special.
Even on a cold day there's a warmth in the spirit.
Call it brotherhood, or peace, or good will.

It is a time to love. A time to give from the heart,
sharing the joys of visiting one another
when we need it most. Warm mugs of spiced tea,
fruit cakes sliced with apples. Sugarplums
dancing in our heads with visions of stockings
filled with more than gifts......filled with the season.

The birth of a baby cries for holding the world
together, in all faiths. A gentle hand reaches
across the world, bringing peace
                    as bright as a silent star.

Afterthoughts

It was months before
the doctors forced me
to realize you were gone.

That dementia sent
you packing in shifts.
We questioned logic:
the why of things
no longer apply.

You were torn from me
like a broken wing—
wounded more than hurt.
They say we must be strong
when you go beyond your
plaque-filled brain into
waves of empty space.

On Seeing My Husband In A Nursing Home

The man on the bed
can't be my husband
Not this shrunken face
less full than mine

I watch him
turn his head
try to speak through
thin-cracked lips
    words
I need to hear

But they die like him
and I think
    they were only
        words

Dr. Skip's Prescription

Studying Mrs. Jackson's file,
I see her mind is sound,
but not her heart or arthritic legs
she measures in defiance
and against the world.
But I can see her knowing
look she sends my way
for reassurance and for more
than what her heart can mend.

She has a right to feel
her life and home are lost
and unrecoverable.
But I prescribe much more
than red and yellow pills.
I suggest her golden years
be moments spent with family
and with friends.
She's not alone. My mother,
unable to communicate,
resides just beyond her door.

We are never alone with ourselves, but with others, we can truly be alone.

Family Dinner Day

Today was Family Dinner Day and half the residents had family members spread throughout the dining room. The smell of pot roast, apple pie, and fresh baked bread filled the room as seniors hugged daughters, sons, husbands, and wives. It was also a joyous time for those who never or rarely visited the Home.

Some of the residents were in wheelchairs unable to speak, while others chatted about their home life. Mrs. Jackson was in her glory when her grandson, Mark, sat on her lap and told her about the new toy he received for his birthday. Randy, the human garbage disposal, stuffed his face with three pieces of apple pie, while Ellen watched his every move and made sure she covered her pot roast with her napkin in case his fingers found her dish.

On the other side of the room, Violet sang with her daughter and Tony to "Achy Breaky," while Fay and George joined in. Agnes still worried about cleaning day, and Willie and Elizabeth sat holding hands by the Christmas tree. And, of course, Andrew sat staring out the window seeing things we only dream about. Most of the nurses and aides introduced themselves to the new visitors, and music and laughter filled the halls.

The only residents unable to attend the dinner were the bed ridden or very ill, who listened from their rooms and watched the colored Christmas lights revolve—like sparklers in the hallway—as Silent Night gently sang them to sleep.

A Home Is Not Always Where The Heart Is

Home For New Years
(if only in my mind)

I feel the wind caressing
me in soft waves, as
the amber clouds scud
across the rolling plains.
A hint of snow frosts the air.
The scent of pine entwines
the bayberry fence where
I slowly close the latch.
A green and red wreathe
hangs against the door.
I feel my hand tremble
grasping the tarnished knob
that once flashed a myriad
of colors across my chest.

Hesitating briefly,
I remember the tired, work-worn hands
that soothed my troubled heart;
the bent, little man who worked
to pay the rent;
three saffron-colored heads busy
with the things children do.
And I wonder how they fared
this New Year's Eve?

Were their hearts filled with peace?
Did they celebrate in silence
by the fire-light glow?

A Home Is Not Always Where The Heart Is

Would they forgive my wandering mind
that took me far away?

A sliver of light caught my eye
as I opened the door.
Two heads bent in thought:
a tree, half lit from the hall,
made me smile
as they raised their heads:
There was joy. There was hope.
They still cared.

A Home Is Not Always Where The Heart Is

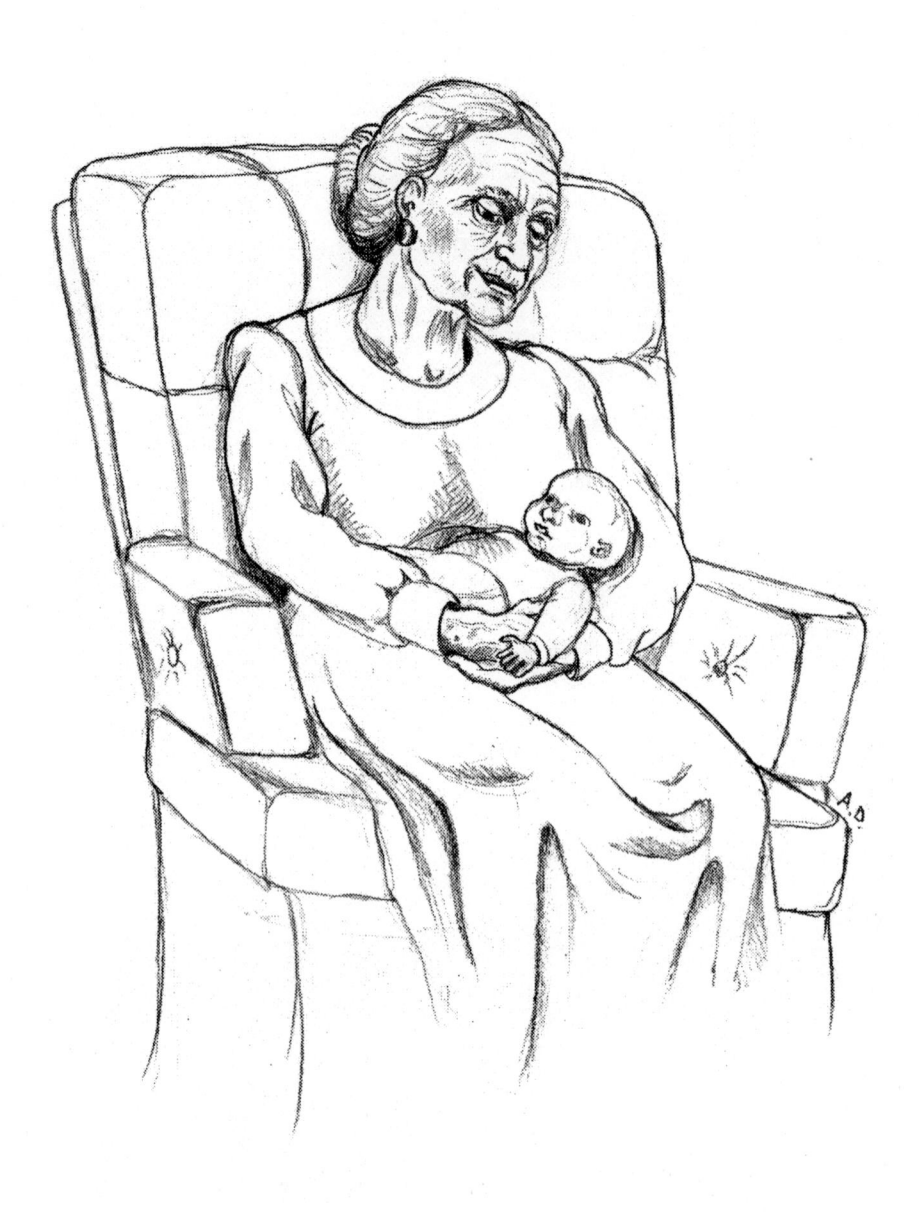

Agnes with her baby doll

If time did not exist, how long would it take to truly grow old?

Mom IV
(daughter speaks)

The phone rang at 9:00 in the evening. It was Anna, the night nurse, at the nursing home. She told me that I had better come over there immediately because Mom had a fall, and it didn't look good. Of course, I rushed out the door, jumped into my car and drove as fast as I could, with thoughts of her dying or ready to be with Dad in my head.

When I arrived, Mom was on oxygen in her bed. At first everyone thought we would lose her, but like all the other times, she bounced back when the aide tried to take her blood pressure. About an hour later she breathed better and slept peacefully. Perhaps her will to live and her gentle spirit gave her the strength to face each new setback even through her dementia.

The next day she was up and walking—just as though nothing had happened, and her appetite for sweets was stronger than ever. Today, the aides and nurses let her sit at the front desk. They give her cookies and listen to her talk about whatever she feels is important.

I think through losing her false teeth, losing weight, refusing to eat or using the toilet anymore, she knows she has much to do on this earth in the way of love. Her greatest lesson. My greatest lesson. A miracle.

Song For Pops
(who passed away in 1996)

Let me sit beside you
on the shore beyond the grave
and learn the secret of the stars.
Let me hold your hand
and feel the rhythm of the night
as beat on beat unites.
Does your new life take you
to our family gone before?
Can you hear their sacred tunes?
Do the delicate sounds of angels
sweeten your lyrical ears?
You who have dreamed and danced
with the throng of earthlings
still sing your metrical songs?
Let me walk your garden path
one last time—
catch the first glint of sun,
and let me touch one final ray
when you sing your hymn,
don silver wings and soar
with the children of tomorrow.

Nursing Home Care

will change in the future.
However, if new horizons are yet to be reached,
it will take a deeper quality
than we are seeing today.
Cooperation will be the catalyst that keeps
the spirit of hope alive for the residents.
Facilities need to come full circle
before we can see a change
from the under-staffed Homes
to the family-related keepers.
It should be the administrator's job
to hire the most dedicated workers.
Learning their craft takes time,
and like any field, the staff
must treat all residents as equals.
To delve into what nursing care really is,
not just the basics. Be ready
for the future of medicine.
Be there to back it up, no matter
what happens or how it changes.
It is a scary thought, this future.
It is up to us, to help them
to be the best they can be.
For the aged are really young at heart,
in any home.

A Home Is Not Always Where The Heart Is
(sitting in my room at the nursing home)

I sit here in silence
and listen for the first
sounds of morning. To
paint a picture with
my mind...through shades.
If I look hard enough, I might see
the live oak stretch its arms
and toss leaves in the breeze.
A bird, a squirrel, or maybe
even a rabbit might circle the tree.
But, mostly, I see the foothills
stretch themselves against the horizon
where shades of red-orange
tinge their purple peaks.
If only I could rise up like those hills
and walk to the farthest side.
It is not enough to describe
what I feel, here, how easy to smell
the rose and step off into
the yellow dawn without getting caught.

Someone, I think, whispers in this room,
"This is your Home."

I lean against the wall where the days
are notched into weeks. Trace the man
I drew from dust. I want to take him

A Home Is Not Always Where The Heart Is

in my arms and caress his face
until we both cry the morning away.
But most of all I want to believe
someone will come to turn up the light.
I'm afraid of this dark and of dying,
to be buried so deep inside,
to never look back to where
my family once lived on the farm,
back then when I was young.
Surely they remember I love them
after all these years.
Together we could beat the odds,
just let me go home.

Afterwords

Dementia is a brain disorder and the most common reason why people are placed in nursing facilities. Alzheimer's disease (AD), which is a form of Dementia, destroys brain cells. No one knows why this happens, but studies indicate that chemistry and the structures of the brain change. And, according to the Alzheimer's Association, one in 10 persons over 65, and nearly half of those over 85, have the disease.

Helping Them:

Ordinary forgetfulness is common with the elderly, but when a person forgets names, dates, or locations of familiar items, and their attention span shortens, concentration is harder, and loss of personal statistics or life memories disappear, this is when drastic measures should be taken for the sake of the individual. The main concern should be to take a serious look at the diagnosis and see what treatments are available.

Once that takes place, steps should be followed to ensure specialized care in all phases of the disease, because as it progresses, people with AD become depressed or anxious and gradually lose their ability to bathe, groom themselves, dress, or use the bathroom. With the demands put on caregivers, and the realization that their loved ones no longer function like they once did, outside help, such as nursing facilities, can relieve some of the burdens and insecurities associated with it.

Today, there are many more care facilities available for adults with disabilities, or those unable to care for themselves, but finding the right place that uniquely approaches the problem is the most important step for the sake of the patients as well as for their families.

While the news media, at times, depicts some nursing homes as "abusive" and "neglectful," there are those that assure us their policies are followed in keeping residents comfortable, cared for 24 hours a day, considerate to their needs, and have healthy and nutritious meals. These are either highly rated by the state or reported on by persons whose loved ones already reside in them.

Once a new resident is admitted in a nursing facility, it is common for them to feel that their lives have been stripped away. They will, in some cases, vent anger at the family and staff. With time, a few will settle in as their fears and anxieties diminish. But, no matter the condition of the resident, their lives have changed, and ours as well.

Another important consideration should be the welfare of the family members. The changes in their lives can be devastating. There needs to be a balancing where spouse, daughter, son, mother, father, grandchild, and other relatives are informed about the person being placed into a care facility. Perhaps having input on different aspects of the resident's care can ease confusion that often occurs.

Helping Us:

Our mental and physical bodies need to be in tune if we are to support the elderly. We need to not just stand back and watch, but be there for them and realize that a family united in aging becomes stronger through education and participation. But at the same time, we need to listen, relax, and understand what is really going on and why. Not all residents in a home have the same problems, but their insecurities and day-to-day living should have as much support as possible.

Everyone—in the life of a resident—can make a difference.

Afterwords

To obtain more information about Alzheimer's disease, contact:

Alzheimer's Association
Phone: (800) 272-3900
Internet Address: **http://www.alz.org**

National Institute on Aging
Phone: (800) 222-2225
Internet Address: **http://www.nih.gov/nia**

National Institute of Neurological
Disorders and Stroke
Internet Address: **http://www.ninds.hih.gov**

A Cure Soon
(Medical News 2002)

A new procedure that may reduce Alzheimer's disease is now in its testing stage, and may be used in five years according to Dr. Mark Tuzynski, director of the Center for Neural Repair at the University of California, San Diego. He predicts that surgery, which consists of implanting modified cells called fibroblasts that outputs nerve growth factor (NGF) would help stop the nerve-cell death associated with Alzheimer's disease.

About the Author

Denise Martinson is a writer and editor/publisher. She is married to Michael Martinson and has two children, Danielle and Michael.

Membership:

The Institute of Noetic Sciences, A. R, E., and The Academy of American Poets.

Studies:

The Newspaper Institute of America, The Institute of Children's Literature, Writer's Digest School, and is currently studying for a certificate from Atlantic University to be a Spiritual Mentor.

Writing credits:

Editor/publisher of *Poetic Page* poetry magazine. Published widely in the poet's market, including work in the children's market. Cited in Anthologies: Who's Who books, newspapers, and individual poetry publications. Listed in *Poets and Writers* of New York. Judged poetry contests for both national and small press publications. Won poetry awards, and has works preserved in the archives at Central Michigan University's Clark Historical Library.

Upcoming Books:

Spiritual in nature.

0-595-26731-9